**Based on the novelization
by Lara Bergen**

**Based on the screenplay by
David Hayter**

LEVEL 1

Adapted by: Paul Shipton

Commissioning Editor: Helen Parker

Editor: Helen Parker

Designer: Susen Vural

Cover layout: Emily Spencer

Picture research: Emma Bree

Photo credits: Cover image and film stills provided
courtesy of Marvel Characters, Inc.

CONTENTS

THE X-MEN

The X-Men are mutants. A mutant is someone with very special powers.

LOGAN

Sometimes people call him Wolverine. He is very strong. He has the special power to heal his body. He has strong metal in his body and metal claws in his hands.

PROFESSOR X

His other name is Charles Xavier. He has a special school for mutants. He can read people's minds. His power is very strong – sometimes he can use his power over people's minds.

ROGUE

She can take the power of other mutants for a short time.

DOCTOR JEAN GREY

She can move things with her mind. She can also read people's minds. She is still learning to use her powers.

THE OTHER MUTANTS

MAGNETO

His other name is Eric Magnus Lensherr. He can move metal things with his mind.

STORM

She has power over the weather. She can make storms, lightening, strong winds …

SABRETOOTH

He is very strong. He is the strongest of all the mutants. He has long teeth and a lot of hair.

MYSTIQUE

She is a blue mutant. She can change to look the same as anyone or anything.

CYCLOPS

The strong beam from his eyes can cut through anything.

TOAD

He is a green mutant. He has a strong and very long tongue.

PLACES

Washington, DC: American politicians meet in this city to talk about their country's problems.
Northern Alberta, Canada: This is where Rogue meets Logan for the first time.
Westchester, New York: Professor X's school for mutants is here.
The Statue of Liberty: This is a famous place near Ellis Island in New York.

CHAPTER 1 'DON'T TOUCH ME!'

'The world is changing,' said Doctor Jean Grey. 'People are changing. No one knows why, but there are more people with special powers.' She looked at the politicians all around her. She was in Washington, DC to tell them about mutants*.

* A mutant is someone with special powers.

Senator Robert Kelly looked at her coldly. 'The important question is this – what can we do about the mutant problem?' He had a paper in his hand. 'These are the names of some mutants here in our country! One girl can walk through walls! Tell me – how can anyone stop her?'

Jean was angry. She tried to speak, but no one listened.

'The mutants are here!' shouted Kelly. 'We must have their names. We must know their powers!'

Kelly's words frightened the other politicians, and they liked his plan.

At the back, a man in a wheelchair left sadly. His name was Charles Xavier or Professor X. As he left he saw an old friend.

'We must still have hope for them, Eric,' said Professor X quietly. 'Humans can change.'

The other man's name was Eric Magnus Lensherr, but he also used the name Magneto. His eyes were hard and cold. 'They *can* change,' he said, ' … into *us*.' He turned to go. 'Humans are not important now, Charles.'

Northern Alberta, Canada. It was late at night. A teenager sat alone in a bar with just water in front of her. She was a long way from home. A man came and asked for a drink. After that he said nothing.

A big man came up behind him. 'You've got some money for me, Wolverine,' he said angrily. The man at the bar still said nothing. The big man turned to go, but then he ran at the man with an angry look in his eyes.

'No!' shouted the teenager, and the man at the bar turned around very fast.

SNIKT! Three long metal claws came out of the back of his hand, close to the big man's face.

And then – SNIKT! – the claws went back into the man's hand. He walked out of the bar. Frightened, the teenager followed him.

It was very cold in the night air. The man got in his car and drove for a while. Then he stopped. Something wasn't right. He looked in the back of the car. The teenager was there.

'What are you doing?' he asked.

'I need help,' said the girl. There was a frightened look in her eyes. The man knew that look, but he liked to be alone.

'Get out,' he said.

'I helped you in the bar!' said the girl.

The man thought about this. A few minutes later, they were both in the car.

'I'm Rogue,' the teenager said as they drove through the empty white country.

'I'm Logan.' He moved to touch her hands. 'You're cold.'

The girl moved her hands away quickly. 'Don't touch

me!' she cried. Then, she said more quietly, 'When people touch me, bad things happen. I have this terrible power. I ran away from home because of it.'

Suddenly, there was a tree in front of them. SMASH! The car hit it and Logan went through the window.

Rogue looked up slowly. Logan's body was face down on the road. 'He must be dead,' she thought.

But no! He started to get up. But how?

'Are you OK?' Logan shouted to Rogue.

'I can't move!' she cried. And now the car was on fire.

Suddenly, a big man with long hair came out of the trees.

Logan tried to use his claws, but the man was very strong. He hit Logan with part of a tree. Logan was face down again on the road.

The big man walked to the car – to Rogue! But then a very strong wind started. The big man with long hair looked around and saw two people – a man and a woman.

Who were they? The woman had white hair. The man had a visor over his eyes. He touched the visor and a red beam came out. It hit the big man and he went down.

The man and the woman opened the car door quickly and helped Rogue out. They were just in time.

Magneto was angry. 'What happened?' he asked.

The big man just said, 'They knew.' His name was Sabretooth and, like Magneto, he was a mutant.

A metal chair moved across the room and Magneto sat down. That was his power – to move metal things with his mind.

'Where is the mutant now?' he asked.

'With *them*,' answered Sabretooth.

Magneto didn't need to ask who. He knew. Logan and Rogue were with Professor X and his team.

CHAPTER 2 THE SCHOOL FOR MUTANTS

Logan was on a table with lights above him. There was a woman in a white coat. It was Doctor Jean Grey.

Logan got up fast and ran out of the door. Where was he? He didn't know.

He went from room to room. He opened a door and looked in at a class. A man in a wheelchair was the teacher. The class finished and the young students started to leave.

'Where am I?' asked Logan.

'Westchester, New York,' answered the teacher. It was Professor X.

'Where's the girl?'

'She's here,' said Professor X. 'She's OK.'

The woman with white hair and the man with the visor came in.

'Meet Storm and Cyclops,' said Professor X. 'They're X-

Men. You came here with them, to my school for mutants. Magneto can't do anything to you here.'

'Who's Magneto?' asked Logan.

'A very strong mutant. He and his friends hate humans. They want you, Logan, but I don't know why.'

Logan laughed. 'This is stupid!'

He started to leave, but Professor X said, 'What happened to you long ago, Logan? You don't remember anything. Am I right? I can help you.'

Logan stopped. Xavier's words were true. He thought about these things all the time. 'What *is* this place?' he asked.

'We all have different powers,' said Professor X. 'I can read people's minds and sometimes I have power over their minds. At this school we help other mutants. We teach them to use their special powers.'

Senator Kelly was on his way home. He talked to one of his men. 'Politicians from over two hundred countries are coming to New York soon. Then we can do something about the mutant problem.'

He looked out of the window. 'Where are we?' he asked.

Suddenly, the man opposite him changed before his eyes. Now he wasn't a man. He was a woman. A blue woman with yellow eyes. A mutant with the power to look the same as anyone.

She hit Kelly very hard. 'I didn't go to school

because of people like *you*!'

Her name was Mystique and she was one of Magneto's mutants. And now they had Senator Kelly.

Jean Grey told the X-Men about her tests on Logan.

'He is very strong and he has the power to heal his body,' she said. 'And there is strong metal all through his body. Someone put it there. They gave him metal claws in both hands, too. Those claws can cut anything.'

'Who did this?' asked Cyclops.

'He doesn't know,' said Jean. 'He remembers nothing.'

Senator Kelly was in a large open room. Mystique was there, and a man with a green face. His name was Toad. Suddenly a very long tongue came out of Toad's mouth. Kelly looked away.

Magneto was behind him. 'You're frightened, Senator Kelly. Frightened because you don't understand us.'

Magneto opened two metal doors with his mind. He walked through the doors and into a big machine.

'What are you going to do to me?' cried Kelly.

The machine started to turn around and around. Magneto closed his eyes – the power for the machine came from him. It almost killed him, but he didn't stop. Then a white light came out of the machine.

'AAARGH!' cried Kelly as the white light moved over him.

Back at Professor X's school, Jean took Logan to his room.

'So what's *your* power?' he asked.

'I can move things with my mind,' said Jean. No one touched them, but the doors behind Logan closed.

'I can also read people's minds,' she said.

Logan moved close to her. 'OK, read my mind,' he said with a smile. 'Or are you too frightened?'

Jean smiled back. 'No,' she said and put her hands on Logan's head.

The pictures came fast and they were terrible. *Logan's body in water … fire … pain … terrible pain …*

Jean took her hands away. Someone was at the door. It was Cyclops.

Jean left the room quickly. 'Good night, Logan,' she said. But Cyclops didn't move.

'What's the problem?' said Logan. 'Are you going to say, "Stay away from my girlfriend."?'

'I don't need to,' said Cyclops. He didn't like Logan much. 'Sabretooth almost killed you and we stopped him. You hate that. Right?'

He turned to go. 'Oh, and, Logan … Stay away from my girlfriend.'

CHAPTER 3 CEREBRO

It was late at night but Rogue wasn't in bed. She liked Professor X's school – the classes and the students – but she was frightened. She wanted to see Logan.

She went quietly into his room. Suddenly, Logan woke up from one of his terrible dreams. He didn't think. There was no time to think. The claws came out of his hands. They went right through Rogue's body.

'No!' he cried.

Their eyes met. Logan looked at his claws. He thought, 'Rogue is going to die.'

His claws went back, but it was too late. 'Help us!' Logan shouted.

The teenager put her hand on his face. She needed to do this. There was no other way. Logan's eyes opened in pain and surprise. His power started to go into Rogue. That was *her* power – when she touched people she took their power.

When the other X-Men arrived Logan was almost dead. Rogue looked at the others. 'I'm sorry,' she said.

Senator Kelly was very frightened. His body was different now because of Magneto's machine. Every day it was more and more like water.

'I must get out of here,' he thought.

The room was in a very tall building with water all around it. He looked out through the bars on his window. His head went easily through the bars. And his body followed quickly after. He started to move down the wall, but suddenly Magneto saw him.

'What did you do to me?' shouted Kelly.

Magneto smiled. 'You are one of us now – a mutant. Who is going to help you?'

Sabretooth tried to take Kelly's hand, but it wasn't possible. Kelly's body was in the air, and then suddenly – SPLASH! Kelly was in the water.

Rogue sat alone in the school gardens. Was Logan OK? She didn't know.

A student called Bobby came to her. He was a teenager too, and Rogue liked him.

'What happened with you and Logan?' said Bobby. '*Never* use your power against other mutants.'

'You don't understand … ' started Rogue, but Bobby didn't listen.

'Leave here,' he said. 'The students are frightened. Professor X is angry. Just go.'

Rogue looked at him sadly. He was right – she must go.
She must always be alone.

'Where's Rogue?' asked Logan. He was OK now
because of his power to heal his body.

Professor X looked into his own mind. 'I can't feel her,'
he said. 'She isn't in the school.'

He went to a small door. The computer by the door
looked into his eyes with a special beam. 'Hello, Professor
X,' it said.

The door opened and he went into a big room. Logan
followed.

'This machine is Cerebro,' said Professor X. 'With
Cerebro my power is very strong. I can use it to find
Rogue.'

'Why not use it to find Magneto?' asked Logan.

'Because Magneto knows Cerebro. He made it with me
a long time ago.'

When Logan left, Professor X put a special helmet on his
head.

Cerebro started to work and he saw lights all around him – thousands of lights. Each light was a person, and they were all mutants. Professor X had a difficult job – to find Rogue out of all those mutants. But his mind was strong. *Very* strong with Cerebro's help. There! He saw her!

'She's at the train station,' he told the X-Men outside. 'Storm and Cyclops, go and find her, please.'

But Logan was already on his way …

Logan took Cyclops' motorbike and arrived very quickly at the station. Rogue was already on a train.

Logan sat down next to her. 'I'm sorry about last night,' he said quietly.

'Me, too.'

'Are you running away again?'

'It's for the best. Professor X is angry with me,' said Rogue.

Logan didn't understand. 'Who said *that*?'

Bobby watched as the other students walked away. When no one was around, he went to a different part of the school – to Cerebro.

Then Bobby started to change. His eyes went yellow and his body went blue. It was Mystique, not Bobby! She went to the door and changed again. Now she had Professor X's face.

The computer used its special beam. 'Hello, Professor X,' it said.

The door opened and Mystique went inside. Now it was easy for her to work on Cerebro.

CHAPTER 4 MAGNETO'S PLAN

The train started with Rogue and Logan still on it.

'My first boyfriend almost died because he touched me,' said Rogue. 'I can still feel him inside my head. I can still feel you …' She started to cry.

Logan thought about this. 'Professor X understands. He wants to help people like us. He wants to help you.'

'OK,' said Rogue.

Cyclops and Storm were at the busy train station, but they weren't alone.

Storm looked around – Sabretooth was behind her! His big arms went around her and he looked into her eyes. 'Cry,' he said. 'I want to hear your pain.'

In a different part of the station, Cyclops turned. He knew something was wrong.

He saw Sabretooth with Storm. But he was too late – Toad was in the station, too. With his long tongue, Toad hit Cyclops' visor. The visor came off his face and the red beam came out of his eyes. Now there was nothing to stop the beam! Cyclops closed his eyes quickly.

Sabretooth still had Storm, but she had power over the weather. Her eyes went white and then the sky went dark. Suddenly, lightning hit right between Sabretooth and Storm. Sabretooth quickly took his arms off Storm and she ran away.

The train stopped very suddenly and the lights went out.

There was a terrible sound as the train's metal walls opened. Then Magneto came in.

Logan was on his feet. SNIKT! His claws were out and ready.

But *metal* claws weren't a problem for Magneto.

'Hello, Wolverine,' he said. He moved his hand. Now it wasn't possible for Logan to move. Magneto moved his hand again and Logan's body went up into the air. Magneto almost pulled Logan's metal claws from his hands. The pain was terrible.

'Stop!' shouted Rogue.

'What … do you want … with me?' said Logan in pain.

'You?' Magneto laughed in surprise. 'I don't want *you*. I want your friend.'

He turned to Rogue. 'And now I have you!'

Back at Westchester, Logan was angry. 'Magneto wanted *me*. You said that.'

'I was wrong,' said Professor X. 'I can't read Magneto's mind any more. He wears a special helmet now to stop me.'

Logan moved to the door.

'Where are you going?' asked Storm.

'I'm going to find Rogue!'

Storm ran after him. 'You can't do this alone, Logan,' she said. 'Help us. Be part of the team.'

Logan stopped. 'Be an X-Man? Don't be stupid! You're a mutant. Humans hate you, but you still want to help them. Maybe Magneto is right …'

He opened the door, but someone was there. It was Senator Kelly. He was almost dead.

'I'm looking for Doctor Jean Grey,' he said.

Minutes later, Senator Kelly was on a table. Professor X was next to him.

'I didn't want to go to a hospital,' said Kelly, 'because I'm a …'

'Mutant?' said Professor X. 'Mutants aren't all bad.'

Kelly's eyes met Xavier's. 'Mutants did this to me.'

Professor X put his hands on Kelly's head. He wanted to look into Kelly's mind and see Magneto's plan. Yes, he saw it all – the big machine, the pain on Magneto's face, the white light …

Professor X told the X-Men everything.

'Magneto's machine can change humans into mutants,' he said. 'But it doesn't work. Senator Kelly is going to die.'

'Why does Magneto want Rogue?' asked Logan.

'The machine's power comes from Magneto. When he

uses it, the machine almost kills him.'

Logan thought carefully about Professor X's words. 'He's going to put his power into Rogue! Then *she* can use the machine. That's his plan!'

CHAPTER 5 THE STATUE OF LIBERTY

Senator Kelly was nearly dead. 'Please don't leave,' he said to Storm. 'I don't want to be alone.'

'OK,' said Storm. She looked at the water on the table. It came from Kelly's body.

'Do you hate humans?' Kelly asked.

'Sometimes I'm frightened of them,' said Storm.

'Don't be frightened of me,' said Kelly. 'Not now.'

And with those last words, his body changed once more. He cried out in pain.

Then suddenly there was just water. Senator Kelly was dead.

Professor X went to Cerebro. He put the helmet on his head. Now he was ready to find Rogue. But Cerebro didn't work – Mystique did something to the machine. A terrible pain hit Professor X. It wasn't possible to think. Then everything went black.

Some of the X-Men found Professor X, but he didn't wake up. Now what? Without him there was no way to find Rogue. Or was there?

Jean went to Cerebro and found the problem quickly. Then she put on the helmet. She was frightened, but it was the only way.

Cyclops was in a different room. He saw Jean with the helmet on. He ran to her, but the door closed.

The pain in Jean's mind was terrible. Her hands went to her head and she cried out.

At last the door opened and Cyclops ran in.

Jean opened her eyes slowly. 'I know Magneto's next move.'

More than two hundred politicians from around the world were in New York. They were there to talk about the world's problems. That night they were at a big party on Ellis Island, near the Statue of Liberty. But Magneto had other ideas. He and his mutants were on a boat near Ellis Island. They had Magneto's machine on it, and they had Rogue, too.

'Are you going to kill me?' Rogue asked.

'Yes,' said Magneto.

'Why?'

'Humans hate us because we are different,' answered Magneto. 'Tonight two hundred of the world's most important people are going to be just like us. They can go home as our brothers … as mutants!'

Sabretooth arrived.

'Put her in the machine,' said Magneto.

The X-Men put on their special black clothes and went in the X-Jet* to New York. Minutes later, the team went through a door into the Statue of Liberty. Everything was very quiet …

* The X-Jet is the X-Men's flying machine.

'Someone's here,' said Logan.

He went and looked in a different room. Then he came back.

'Someone's here,' Logan said again. Then he put out his claws … and ran at Cyclops! Suddenly, a second Logan ran into the first. The first one wasn't Logan – it was Mystique in Logan's shape!

Now both Logans had their claws out. The X-Men wanted to help, but how? Which was the true Logan?

Suddenly, Toad was there, too. He hit the other X-Men to the floor. Then he closed a metal door with his long tongue. Cyclops and Jean were in that room.

In a different room, Logan and Mystique hit each other. She was fast and strong, but Logan was faster and stronger. Mystique knew it and she ran off into the dark.

Then Toad hit Storm in the face and then the body. He laughed – this was easy. But then Storm's eyes went white. It was time to use her weather power. The wind hit Toad very hard. SMASH! He went through a window. He didn't fly out into the night because he put his tongue around something.

Suddenly – ZZZKKKKT! Lighting hit the mutant and he went up into the air with a cry of pain.

Logan waited alone at the foot of the Statue of Liberty. Storm came up behind him.

'Is that you, Logan?' she asked. 'We must find the others.'

'There's a problem,' said Logan. 'You're not part of the team.'

He turned quickly and his claws went into Storm's body. It wasn't Storm – it was Mystique in a new shape! As the pain hit her, she changed back to her true shape.

Logan looked down at her. Was she dead? He didn't know.

Cyclops and Jean were out now, thanks to Cyclops' beam. They found Logan, and then Storm. At last the X-Men were together again. They started the long walk to the top of the Statue of Liberty, up to Magneto and his machine.

CHAPTER 6 'THE WORLD IS GOING TO BE OURS!'

The X-Men arrived at the head of the Statue of Liberty. Logan stopped. He told the others, 'Get out! I can't move.'

Suddenly, bits of metal went around the X-Men's arms, and around their legs. It wasn't possible to move.

And then Magneto was there. 'Hello, my brother mutants,' he said.

Sabretooth ran in and took the visor from Cyclops' face. Cyclops closed his eyes. He must not open them – Jean was right in front of him.

'I saw Senator Kelly,' Jean told Magneto. 'He's dead now. Your machine doesn't work. It kills people!'

But Magneto didn't listen. He didn't want to stop now. 'Those politicians down there have power over us and every mutant in the world. Soon *they* are going to be mutants, too.'

He used his power to fly up to the very top of the Statue of Liberty. His machine was there. And Rogue was in it.

'Help me!' she shouted.

Magneto went into the machine.

'I'm sorry,' he said to Rogue.

Logan had a plan, but not an easy one. He needed to cut through the metal around him. SNIKT! His claws came out. They went right through the metal … and through Logan's body, too.

Sabretooth looked down at Logan. Was he dead?

No! Logan's power was strong. He got up fast and hit Sabretooth with his claws. Now the two mutants were face to face again. They started this back in Canada. Now it was time to finish it.

Up at the machine, Magneto put his hands on Rogue. His power went into Rogue. Then he turned the machine on. They both cried out in pain.

Logan's claws moved like lightning, but no one was stronger than Sabretooth. He hit Logan, and the X-Man almost went flying out of the Statue of Liberty. Only his claws stopped him.

But Logan saw something near to his hand now – Cyclops' visor. Jean saw this, too.

With the power of her mind, she moved the visor fast to Cyclop's face.

'Open your eyes now!' she shouted to Cyclops. The red beam came out and hit Sabretooth. It hit him right out of the Statue of Liberty and into the night. His body didn't hit the water. It hit Magneto's boat. Sabretooth wasn't a problem now!

With Rogue's power the machine turned around faster and faster. Magneto waited near the machine. 'Soon,' he thought, 'the world is going to be ours!'

The X-Men looked up at Magneto's machine.

'Can you hit it with your beam, Cyclops?' asked Logan.

'Not with Rogue in it.' Cyclops turned to Storm. 'Can I go up there with your wind power?'

'Let me go,' said Logan, 'Then you can use your beam from here.'

Storm started to use her power. A strong wind took Logan up into the air. Jean helped with her mind power. Logan almost went over the top of the machine, but he put his hand on it. He was there!

A white light came from the machine. Logan's claws were out and ready. But some of Magneto's power was back now. He stopped Logan's metal claws with his mind. Logan tried and tried to move, but it wasn't possible.

The light from the machine was bigger and bigger. And it moved nearer to the politicians on Ellis Island.

The other X-Men watched. Cyclops didn't want to hit Rogue or Logan. He waited and waited … 'Now!'

The red beam went up and hit Magneto on the back. Then, Logan cut the machine with his claws. There was no more white light. It was finished.

But what about Rogue? Logan looked down into her eyes. She was almost dead. There was only one thing to do

– give his power to her.

Logan put his hands on her face. At first nothing happened. Then, very slowly Rogue came back to life.

The X-Men were back in Westchester.

Logan opened his eyes. Jean Grey was there.

'How's Rogue?' he asked.

'She's OK,' smiled Jean. 'I think she likes you.'

Their eyes met. 'You can tell her this,' said Logan. 'I love a different person.'

Jean knew this, but Cyclops was her boyfriend.

'But …' Jean started.

Logan didn't want to hear. 'How's Professor X?' he asked quickly.

Professor X was OK now, and he was ready to help Logan.

'Go to Lake Alkali in Canada,' he said. 'Maybe you can find some answers there. You can learn who you are.'

'Thank you,' said Logan quietly.

Rogue saw Logan as he left the school. She left her friends and ran to him.

'Please don't go,' she said.

Logan smiled. 'It's OK. I'm coming back.'

Magneto was in a special place. There was no metal in the walls, no metal in the chairs or table. There was no way to use his power here, and no way to get out.

But Magneto was not alone that day.

'Why do you come here?' he asked his old friend,

Charles Xavier. 'Oh, I know. You're still looking for hope.'
There was no hope in Magneto's eyes.

He watched as Professor X left. 'This isn't the end,
Charles,' he said. 'This place can't keep me. I'm going to
give mutants the power over the world.'

'And I'm going to be there, ready for you, old friend,'
said Professor X quietly.

THE X-MEN COMIC

The film, *X-Men*, came out in 2000, but the team is much older. The X-Men were first in a comic from Marvel in 1963. Stan Lee was the writer and Jack Kirby was the artist. Lee and Kirby started many of the most famous super-hero comics – *Spider-Man*, the *Fantastic Four*, the *Incredible Hulk* ...

The front of an X-Men comic

WERE THE FIRST X-MEN THE SAME AS IN THE FILM?

Professor X put the first team of mutants together, and Cyclops and Jean Grey were there. But the other X-Men were different. In the first comic, the X-Men were also against Magneto and his bad mutants.

HOW WERE THE X-MEN DIFFERENT FROM OTHER COMICS?

The X-Men were teenagers with teenagers' problems. At first they didn't know how to use their powers. Professor X wanted to teach and help them. Most humans hated mutants and were frightened of these super-heroes.

WHY DID THE TEAM CHANGE?

Marvel ended the first comic of the X-Men in 1969. Many readers loved the comic, but more people read other super-hero comics like *Spider-Man*.

But Marvel didn't forget the X-Men. They decided to bring the team back in 1975. This time the X-Men were different. Jean Grey, Cyclops and Professor X were still there, but the new team also had Logan (Wolverine), Storm, and other new mutants with very different powers. And they weren't all from America. Storm was from Africa. A mutant called Colossus was from Russia.

'STAN THE MAN'

Many people think Stan Lee is the 'father' of super-hero comics. He likes to be in the films of his comics. In *X-Men*, when Senator Kelly comes out of the water, Stan Lee is near the hot dog stand..

THE BIGGEST COMIC IN THE WORLD

More and more people read the new X-Men comic. Soon writer Chris Claremont started to work on the comic. He worked on *X-Men* for around 15 years and wrote many of the most famous stories.

Logan and his claws quickly became the readers' favourite. Sometimes there were stories just about Logan.

Logan in the X-Men comic

In the 1980s, Marvel made more comics about Professor X and his school for mutants:

- *The New Mutants* was about a team of young students at the school in Westchester. This team later became X-Force.

- *X-Factor* put the old X-Men from the first comic back in the team.

- *Excalibur* put some British super-heroes into a team of mutants.

The X-Men changed a lot over the years. Some mutants left the team and new ones arrived. Some died – and some died and came back to life. There was even a change in Magneto. He became good and worked with the X-Men for a while!

Over the years, people bought over 400 million X-Men comics! And the comic was in twenty-two different languages. It is maybe the biggest super-hero comic in the world!

Do you read super-hero comics?
Which is your favourite?

What do these words mean? You can use a dictionary.
comic   artist   super-hero   hot dog stand   became (*past* of become)

THE FILM

Marvel Comics wanted to make a film of the X-Men for a long time. But they needed the new computer effects of the 1990s to tell the story well. The cost of the film was $75 million. It came out in 2000, and was one of the big hits of the summer. It made $294 million in cinemas around the world.

The director, Bryan Singer

WHO WAS THE DIRECTOR?

The director of the film was Bryan Singer. He liked the idea of this super-hero film. For him, the story has an important lesson. It teaches people: 'Don't hate others because they are different.'

Have you seen the film *X-Men*? Did you like it? Do you want to be a super-hero?

WHO WROTE THE FILM?

Tom de Santo and director Bryan Singer wrote the story. David Hayter wrote the script. All three men also have small parts in the film – as policemen with no words!

WHERE DID THEY MAKE THE FILM?

They made the film in Canada, in and around Toronto. They even made a model of the top of the Statue of Liberty there.

IS THE FILM THE SAME AS THE COMIC?

The film is true to the X-Men comic and its ideas. But some things are different …

THE COMIC	THE FILM
Before she comes to the X-Men, Rogue is a bad mutant.	Rogue runs away from home because she is frightened of her power.
Rogue is much stronger because she took powers from a super-hero and she kept them. In the comic Rogue can fly.	When Rogue takes someone's powers, they do not stay in her for very long.
Bobby Drake (Iceman) was in the first team of X-Men from the 1960s.	Bobby Drake is just a student at Professor X's school.
The X-Men usually wear special yellow clothes.	The X-Men wear special black clothes. (But after the film came out the X-Men in the comic also started to wear black.)
Jean Grey uses her super-hero name Marvel Girl. She later becomes Phoenix.	Jean Grey does not use a special super-hero name.

Jean Grey in the comic.

Jean Grey in the film.

Most readers of the comic loved the film. After *X-Men*, there were other great films of Marvel super-heroes – *Spider-Man*, *Hulk*, *Daredevil* and *The Fantastic Four*.

What do these words mean?
You can use a dictionary.

effects   director   super-hero   script
model   comic   kept (*past* of keep)

THE STATUE OF LIBERTY

Some of the most exciting parts of the X-Men film happen in the Statue of Liberty. Magneto takes Rogue to the very top of the statue. There he tries to use Rogue's power to change humans into mutants.

The Statue of Liberty is of course a very famous place. For many people it is a symbol of New York and of the USA.

WHERE IS THE STATUE?

It is on Liberty Island in New York Harbor. A long time ago, people arrived in New York by boat. The Statue of Liberty was the first thing they saw.

HOW DID IT COME TO NEW YORK?

The French gave the statue to the people of the USA. It arrived in New York on 17th June 1885. It arrived on a boat in 214 boxes. They took four months to put together the statue on Bedloe's Island (now Liberty Island).

WHO WAS THE DESIGNER?

Frederic-Auguste Bartholdi was the main designer. Gustave Eiffel designed the framework (he designed the Eiffel Tower in Paris).

> What do you think is a symbol of your country? What do you know about this symbol?

WHAT DID THEY USE TO MAKE THE STATUE?

They used metal for the framework, then they put copper on top. When it is new, copper is red. After some time, it goes green. This is why the statue is green.

FUN FACTS

● It is 93 metres high and the right arm is almost 13 metres long.

● The statue has a 'book' in her left hand. On the 'book' there are the words: JULY IV MDCCLXXVI (July 4th 1776 – American Independence Day).

● The American people gave a small Statue of Liberty to the French in 1889. You can see it in Paris by the Seine:

What do these words mean?
You can use a dictionary.

symbol island box design /
designer framework copper

CHAPTERS 1–2

Before you read

You can use your dictionary for these questions.

1 Match the words on the left with the words on the right.

a)	beam	i	mouth
b)	kill	ii	thought
c)	mind	iii	hand
d)	touch	iv	light
e)	tongue	v	dead

2 Use these words to complete the sentences.

   cut   heal   human   machines   metal   politician

   a) A good ... works to help people in his or her country.
   b) A computer and a television are both ... .
   c) We make things out of ... because it is strong.
   d) I went to the doctor when I ... my hand.
   e) He can ... people with his hands.
   f) All people are ... .

3 Look at People and Places on pages 4–5.
   a) Who has **claws**?
   b) Who has a **visor** over his eyes?
   c) Who is in a **wheelchair**?
   d) Who has **power** over the weather?

After you read

4 Answer the questions.
   a) Why is Jean Grey in Washington, DC?
   b) Why did Rogue run away from home?
   c) Who gets Rogue out of the car?
   d) Who has a school in Westchester, New York?
   e) What does Jean learn about Logan's body?
   f) What is Jean's power?

5 What do you think?
  a) Why does Magneto want Logan and Rogue?
  b) What is going to happen to Senator Kelly?

CHAPTERS 3–4

Before you read
You can use a dictionary for these questions.
  6 Match the words and the sentences.
  air   helmet   lightning   pain   shape
  a) You put this on your head.
  b) You need this to live.
  c) This is the outline of something.
  d) It comes from the sky in a storm. It can kill.
  e) A doctor can give you something to help this.

After you read
  7 Put these events in order.
  a) Logan finds Rogue on a train.
  b) Logan almost kills Rogue.
  c) Magneto takes Rogue.
  d) Mystique goes to Cerebro.
  e) Professor X uses Cerebro to find Rogue.
  f) Rogue runs away from the school.

  8 Choose the correct answer.
  a) Magneto is planning to …
    kill humans / change humans into mutants.
  b) Senator Kelly comes to the school because …
    he was frightened to go to a hospital / he is a friend
    of Jean Grey.
  c) Magneto has Rogue because …
    he wants her to use the machine / he wants to use
    the machine on her.

  9 Do you think Logan is going to be one of the X-Men?

CHAPTERS 5–6

Before you read

10 All of these things happen in chapters 5–6. Think about the answers.

   a) Who dies at the school?
   b) Who uses Cerebro to find Magneto and Rogue?
   c) Who does Magneto want to turn into mutants?
   d) Logan and Sabretooth meet again. What happens?

11 Who is going to say these words?

   a) 'Do you hate humans?'
   b) 'Are you going to kill me?'
   c) 'Soon the world is going to be ours.'
   d) 'And I am going to be there, ready for you, old friend.'

After you read

12 Correct these sentences.

   a) Professor X uses Cerebro to find Magneto.
   b) Over two hundred mutants meet near the Statue of Liberty.
   c) Cyclops gives his power to Rogue.
   d) Rogue dies.

13 What do you think?

   a) Who is your favourite mutant in the story? Why?
   b) At the start of the book, Professor X says, 'Humans can change.' Is this true?
   c) You are a mutant. What special power would you like?

14 You are a student at Professor X's school. Write a letter to tell new students about the school.